HUBSPOT USER GUIDE

Comprehensive Gide from Beginner to Pro | Boost Your Marketing Skills

Felicia D. Sandridge

CONTENTS

PREFACE

Welcome to the "HubSpot User Guide"! This book aims to serve as a comprehensive companion for individuals, professionals, and businesses seeking to harness the full potential of HubSpot's powerful suite of tools and resources.

In today's digital landscape, effective marketing, sales, and customer service strategies are integral to success. HubSpot stands as a robust solution, offering a plethora of features designed to streamline workflows, enhance customer interactions, and drive growth. Whether you're a seasoned marketer, a sales representative, or a business owner looking to expand your online presence, this guide is crafted to provide you with the insights and knowledge needed to navigate the HubSpot platform effectively.

This book is structured to cater to users at varying levels of familiarity with HubSpot, from beginners seeking fundamental understanding to experienced users aiming to optimize their strategies. Throughout these pages, you'll find step-by-step instructions, practical tips, and real-world examples to help you leverage HubSpot's functionalities to their fullest potential.

It's important to note that the digital landscape is ever-evolving, and while every effort has been made to ensure the accuracy and relevance of the information presented herein, changes and updates to the HubSpot platform may occur. Therefore, I encourage readers to supplement this guide with the latest resources available through HubSpot's official documentation and updates.

I extend my gratitude to the team at HubSpot for creating a dynamic platform that empowers businesses worldwide, and to the readers who have chosen this guide to deepen their understanding and expertise in utilizing HubSpot.

I hope this book serves as a valuable resource on your journey to mastering HubSpot and achieving your marketing, sales, and customer service objectives.

Best regards.

INTRODUCTION

*Understanding the
Importance of HubSpot*

C ustomer service efforts. Its significance lies in its comprehensive approach to inbound marketing, offering a suite of interconnected tools that enable companies to attract, engage, and delight customers. Let's delve into the importance of HubSpot through various lenses:

Centralized Data Management

One of the paramount aspects of HubSpot is its ability to centralize data across various business functions. **Centralized data management** ensures that all customer interactions, from website visits to email engagements, are recorded in one place. This single source of truth allows for a holistic view of customer behavior, enabling businesses to tailor their strategies effectively.

Seamless Marketing Automation

HubSpot's marketing automation capabilities empower businesses to automate repetitive tasks and nurture leads effectively. **Automated workflows** streamline the marketing process by triggering specific actions based on user behavior, ensuring timely and personalized interactions with prospects. This level of automation frees up valuable time for marketers to focus on strategy and creativity.

Integrated Sales CRM

The platform's **integrated CRM** (Customer Relationship Management) system serves as a unified hub for sales teams. It facilitates lead tracking, manages contacts, and provides insights into the sales pipeline. This integration allows for better collaboration between marketing and sales teams, ensuring a smoother transition of leads and a more efficient sales process.

Robust Analytics and Reporting

HubSpot's analytics and reporting tools provide **in-depth insights** into the performance of marketing campaigns, sales activities, and customer interactions. From tracking website traffic to monitoring email open rates, businesses can leverage data-driven decisions to optimize their strategies continually. This analytics suite aids in identifying strengths, weaknesses, and areas for improvement.

Personalization and Customization

The platform offers **personalization features** that enable businesses to tailor their content and communication based on individual preferences and behaviors. By creating targeted content and personalized interactions, companies can enhance engagement and foster stronger relationships with their audience, leading to higher conversion rates and customer loyalty.

Scalability and Flexibility

HubSpot's scalability makes it suitable for businesses of all sizes. Whether a startup or an enterprise-level corporation, the platform offers **flexibility in scaling** its services according to the specific needs and growth trajectory of a business. This adaptability allows companies to evolve their strategies without worrying about outgrowing the platform.

Streamlined Customer Service

Beyond marketing and sales, HubSpot's features extend to **customer service**. It provides tools for managing customer inquiries, ticketing systems, and knowledge bases. This holistic approach ensures a seamless customer experience throughout the entire lifecycle, leading to increased satisfaction and loyalty.

Brief Overview Of Hubspot's Features And Capabilities

HubSpot is a multifaceted platform that combines a range of features and capabilities to facilitate inbound marketing strategies. **Let's explore some of its key functionalities in detail:**

Content Management System (CMS)

The HubSpot CMS enables businesses to create and manage engaging content for their websites. With **built-in SEO tools** and a user-friendly interface, users can design and optimize web pages without extensive technical knowledge. The CMS's drag-and-drop functionality simplifies content creation and ensures a responsive design across devices.

Email Marketing and Automation

HubSpot's **email marketing tools** empower users to design, send, and track email campaigns efficiently. The platform offers customizable templates, A/B testing, and automated workflows to nurture leads and engage with contacts at various stages of the buyer's journey. Detailed analytics help in refining email strategies for better engagement.

Social Media Management

Businesses can manage their social media presence effectively using HubSpot's **social media tools**. Users can schedule posts, monitor mentions, and analyze social performance within the platform. Integration with other marketing efforts allows for a cohesive strategy across multiple channels.

Lead Generation and Management

HubSpot facilitates **lead generation** through forms, pop-ups, and live chat features embedded on websites. The platform captures visitor information and segments leads based on their behavior and demographics. Lead scoring and nurturing tools assist in identifying and prioritizing high-potential leads for conversion.

Sales Hub

The Sales Hub component of HubSpot provides a suite of tools for **sales teams**. It includes features for pipeline management, email tracking, meeting scheduling, and performance analytics. The CRM allows sales professionals to track interactions and manage deals efficiently.

Service Hub

The Service Hub focuses on **customer support and service**. It offers tools for ticketing, knowledge base creation, live chat, and customer feedback collection. This centralized approach helps businesses provide timely and personalized support to enhance customer satisfaction.

GETTING STARTED WITH HUBSPOT

*Creating an Account
and Setting Up*

C reating an account and setting up on a platform like HubSpot is crucial for efficient use. To begin, the initial step involves accessing the HubSpot website and clicking on the "Get Started" or "Sign Up" button. This will prompt you to fill in essential details like email, name, company name, and password. Once the basic information is entered, it's pivotal to verify the email address used for the account creation. This might involve clicking on a verification link sent to the provided email. After verification, users are often directed to set up their account by providing additional details like company size, industry, goals, and challenges.

Moreover, **account setup might involve selecting a subscription plan**, depending on the features required. HubSpot usually offers various plans catering to different business needs, such as Marketing Hub, Sales Hub, Service

Hub, and CRM. **Selecting the right plan is vital as it determines the tools and functionalities accessible.** After choosing a plan, **users might be asked to connect their social media accounts, import contacts, or integrate with other software for seamless data synchronization.** This integration step is essential for maximizing HubSpot's capabilities in managing customer relationships.

Navigating The Hubspot Dashboard

The HubSpot dashboard is a comprehensive control center designed to streamline various marketing, sales, and service processes. **Upon logging in, users are directed to the dashboard, which is the central hub for accessing different tools and features.** It typically consists of multiple sections, each tailored to specific functionalities like marketing analytics, sales pipelines, customer support, and more.

One prominent feature often visible on the dashboard is the "Quick Access Toolbar", which allows easy navigation to frequently used tools or reports. **The navigation bar usually contains tabs like "Contacts," "Marketing," "Sales," and "Service." Clicking on these tabs directs users to specific modules relevant to those categories.** For instance, clicking on the "Marketing" tab may lead to tools for creating campaigns, analyzing performance, and managing content.

Another crucial aspect of navigating the dashboard involves customizing it according to individual preferences. This can include rearranging widgets, adding shortcuts to frequently used features, or creating personalized reports for quick access to essential metrics. Moreover, **utilizing the search bar within the dashboard can significantly aid in quickly finding specific tools or functionalities**.

Understanding Hubspot's Interface

Understanding the interface of HubSpot involves grasping the layout, design, and functionality of its various sections. **The interface is typically user-friendly, designed with intuitive elements for easier navigation and use. The primary interface often consists of a sidebar with tabs for different functionalities.** For instance, the "Marketing" section might encompass tools for email marketing, content creation, analytics, and automation.

Each tab within the interface usually contains sub-sections or modules. For instance, under the "Marketing" tab, there might be options for creating email campaigns, managing social media, analyzing website traffic, and more. **Users can navigate through these sections by clicking on the desired tool or module.** Furthermore, **HubSpot's interface often integrates visual elements like graphs, charts, and reports to present data in a comprehensible manner.**

One key aspect to note is the responsiveness of the interface, which means it adapts well to different screen sizes and devices. This ensures a consistent user experience across various platforms such as desktops, tablets, or mobile phones. **Additionally, understanding how to access support resources within the interface, such as help documentation, tutorials, or customer support, is crucial for effective usage.**

MASTERING THE BASICS

Managing Contacts and Companies

Managing contacts and companies efficiently is crucial for any business looking to streamline its operations and improve customer relationships. In today's digital age, utilizing Customer Relationship Management (CRM) systems like HubSpot can greatly enhance these efforts.

Key Aspects of Contact Management:

1. **Centralized Database:** A CRM platform like HubSpot offers a centralized database to store all contact information, including names, emails, phone numbers, and interaction history. This allows for easy access and reference.

2. **Segmentation and Tagging:** Users can segment contacts based on various criteria like demographics, behavior, or purchase history. Tagging contacts with specific attributes allows for targeted marketing and personalized communication.

3. **Automated Communication:** Automation

features in HubSpot enable the scheduling of emails, follow-ups, and reminders, ensuring timely and consistent communication with contacts.

4. **Customization and Personalization:** Tailoring interactions based on individual preferences and behaviors helps in building stronger relationships. HubSpot's customization options enable personalized content delivery.

5. **Integration Capabilities:** HubSpot integrates with various applications and tools, enabling seamless data flow between different systems, thus enhancing efficiency.

Benefits of Effective Company Management:

1. **Streamlined Processes:** Efficient management of company profiles in HubSpot helps in organizing and structuring business interactions, leading to streamlined processes.

2. **Improved Customer Service:** Detailed company profiles facilitate a deeper understanding of client needs and preferences, enabling businesses to provide more personalized and effective customer service.

3. **Enhanced Sales Opportunities:** By tracking and analyzing company data, sales teams can identify potential leads, understand their requirements, and tailor their approach to increase conversion rates.

4. **Data-Driven Decision Making:** Access to

comprehensive company data aids in making informed decisions regarding marketing strategies, sales targets, and resource allocation.

5. **Scalability and Growth:** Proper management of company profiles lays the groundwork for scalable growth by identifying areas for expansion and focusing efforts on promising opportunities.

Utilizing Hubspot's Marketing Tools

HubSpot's marketing tools offer a wide array of functionalities designed to empower businesses in reaching their target audience, nurturing leads, and driving conversions.

Effective Use of HubSpot's Marketing Tools:

1. **Content Creation and Management:** HubSpot's content creation tools enable the creation and management of engaging content such as blog posts, emails, social media posts, and landing pages. Utilizing these tools helps in attracting and retaining customers.

2. **Email Marketing Automation:** Leveraging HubSpot's email marketing automation allows for personalized and timely communication with leads and customers. Segmentation and smart workflows enhance the effectiveness of email campaigns.

3. **SEO Optimization:** HubSpot provides tools for Search Engine Optimization (SEO) that help businesses improve their website's visibility in search engine results. These tools aid in keyword

research, on-page optimization, and content strategy.

4. **Social Media Management:** The platform offers social media management tools for scheduling posts, monitoring engagement, and analyzing performance across various social media channels.

5. **Analytics and Reporting:** HubSpot's analytics capabilities provide insights into the performance of marketing campaigns, helping in measuring ROI, identifying successful strategies, and making data-driven decisions.

Benefits of Leveraging HubSpot's Marketing Tools:

1. **Increased Efficiency:** The integration of various marketing tools within HubSpot saves time and effort by centralizing marketing operations, allowing for smoother execution of campaigns.

2. **Enhanced Lead Nurturing:** Effective use of marketing tools facilitates targeted and personalized communication with leads, nurturing them through the sales funnel more effectively.

3. **Improved Campaign Effectiveness:** Detailed analytics and reporting help in evaluating the success of marketing efforts, enabling marketers to optimize campaigns for better results.

4. **Better Customer Insights:** The tools provide valuable insights into customer behavior, preferences, and engagement patterns, aiding in

crafting more relevant and impactful marketing strategies.

5. **Consistent Branding and Messaging:** Utilizing HubSpot's tools ensures consistency in branding and messaging across various channels, strengthening brand identity and recognition.

Exploring Sales And Crm In Hubspot

Sales and CRM functionalities in HubSpot play a pivotal role in managing leads, tracking sales activities, and fostering customer relationships.

Crucial Features in Sales and CRM:

1. **Lead Management:** HubSpot's CRM allows for efficient lead management, tracking interactions, and organizing leads based on their stage in the sales pipeline.

2. **Pipeline Management:** It offers customizable sales pipelines to visualize and manage deals, enabling sales teams to track progress and prioritize tasks effectively.

3. **Task Automation:** Automation features streamline repetitive tasks, allowing sales representatives to focus on more critical activities like engaging with leads and closing deals.

4. **Sales Analytics:** Detailed analytics provide insights into sales performance, allowing teams to identify bottlenecks, assess conversion rates, and optimize strategies.

5. **Integration with Marketing:** Seamless integration between sales and marketing tools facilitates alignment between departments, ensuring a cohesive approach towards customer engagement.

Benefits of Sales and CRM in HubSpot:

1. **Improved Sales Efficiency:** Streamlined processes and automation tools in HubSpot's CRM reduce administrative tasks, enabling sales teams to concentrate on revenue-generating activities.

2. **Enhanced Collaboration:** Centralized data and communication within the CRM foster collaboration among sales teams, leading to better coordination and shared goals.

3. **Better Customer Relationships:** Comprehensive customer profiles and interaction history aid in understanding customer needs and preferences, enabling personalized interactions and stronger relationships.

4. **Informed Decision Making:** Access to real-time data and analytics empowers sales teams to make data-driven decisions, leading to more effective sales strategies and higher conversion rates.

5. **Scalability and Growth:** The scalability of HubSpot's CRM allows businesses to adapt and grow, accommodating increased sales volumes and expanding customer bases effectively.

Effectively managing contacts, leveraging marketing tools, and exploring sales and CRM functionalities in HubSpot are critical aspects of modern businesses aiming for growth and sustained success. By understanding and harnessing these capabilities, organizations can streamline operations, nurture customer relationships, and drive revenue generation more effectively.

ADVANCED FEATURES AND STRATEGIES

*Implementing Workflows
and Automation*

Workflows and automation play pivotal roles in streamlining processes, reducing errors, and enhancing productivity across various industries. Implementing workflows involves designing a systematic sequence of tasks that defines how work should be accomplished, ensuring efficiency and consistency. Businesses often adopt workflow automation to automate repetitive tasks, minimize manual intervention, and expedite project completion.

One key aspect is **identifying repetitive tasks** within an organization. This could include data entry, email responses, or document approvals. By recognizing these tasks, businesses can effectively streamline their workflows by automating these processes. **Automating**

routine tasks frees up valuable time for employees, allowing them to focus on more complex and high-value assignments, thereby boosting overall productivity.

Another critical element is **choosing the right automation tools**. There's a wide array of workflow automation software available, ranging from simple task management tools to complex enterprise-level solutions. **Considerations when selecting automation tools** include scalability, ease of integration with existing systems, customizability, and cost-effectiveness. For instance, platforms like Zapier, Microsoft Power Automate, or custom-built solutions tailored to specific business needs can significantly enhance workflow efficiency.

Testing and refining workflows are integral to successful implementation. Initially, it's essential to run pilot tests or simulations to ensure the automated workflows function as intended. This phase allows for necessary adjustments and refinements before full deployment. Continuous monitoring and periodic evaluations ensure workflows remain effective and adaptable to evolving business needs.

Optimizing Sales Processes with Advanced CRM Tools

Sales processes form the backbone of any successful business, and leveraging advanced Customer Relationship Management (CRM) tools can significantly boost sales efficiency. **Optimizing sales processes** involves utilizing CRM tools to manage customer interactions, track leads, and streamline sales pipelines for enhanced performance and better decision-making.

One key benefit of using CRM tools is **centralizing customer data**. These platforms enable businesses to consolidate customer information, including contact details, purchase history, preferences, and communication logs, into a single database. This centralized repository facilitates a deeper understanding of customers, enabling personalized interactions and targeted marketing strategies.

Automating lead management is another critical aspect of optimizing sales processes. CRM systems often offer functionalities to automate lead capturing, routing, and nurturing. By setting up automated workflows for lead qualification and follow-ups, sales teams can efficiently manage and prioritize leads, ultimately increasing conversion rates and revenue.

Utilizing analytics and reporting features within CRM tools is crucial for data-driven decision-making. Advanced CRM platforms offer robust analytics capabilities, providing insights into sales performance, forecasting trends, and identifying opportunities for improvement. Leveraging these insights allows businesses to make informed strategic decisions and adapt sales strategies for optimal results.

Harnessing The Power Of Analytics And Reporting

Analytics and reporting are indispensable tools for businesses seeking to gain valuable insights into their operations, customer behaviors, and market trends. **Harnessing the power of analytics** involves leveraging data analysis techniques and reporting tools to derive actionable insights for informed decision-making and strategic planning.

One fundamental aspect is **defining clear objectives** for data analysis. Before diving into analytics, businesses must identify specific goals they aim to achieve through data insights. Whether it's optimizing marketing campaigns, improving operational efficiency, or understanding customer behavior, having clear objectives ensures focused and meaningful analysis.

Collecting and consolidating data from various sources is crucial for comprehensive analytics. Businesses gather data from diverse channels such as websites, social media, customer interactions, sales transactions, and more. Aggregating this data into a unified database allows for a holistic view, enabling better analysis and reporting.

Utilizing advanced analytics techniques such as predictive analytics, machine learning, and data visualization can uncover deeper insights. Predictive analytics helps forecast future trends, machine learning algorithms identify patterns within vast datasets, and data visualization tools present complex data in easily understandable formats, facilitating quicker decision-making.

Moreover, **interpreting and acting upon insights** derived from analytics is paramount. Businesses must not only analyze data but also translate findings into actionable strategies. Whether it's adjusting marketing campaigns, refining product offerings, or optimizing operational processes, implementing changes based on data-driven insights is crucial for business growth and success.

INTEGRATIONS AND CUSTOMIZATIONS

Integrating HubSpot with Other Platforms

I ntegrating HubSpot with other platforms is a strategic approach that allows businesses to streamline their operations, enhance efficiency, and maximize their marketing efforts. Some key points to consider when integrating HubSpot with other platforms include:

1. **Identifying Integration Objectives:** Before integrating HubSpot with other platforms, it's crucial to define specific objectives. Determine what you aim to achieve through integration, whether it's syncing data, automating processes, or enhancing customer experience.

2. **Choosing Compatible Platforms:** Select platforms that align with your business goals and are compatible with HubSpot. Whether it's CRM systems like Salesforce, eCommerce platforms

such as Shopify, or email marketing tools like Mailchimp, ensure seamless integration capabilities.

3. **Data Synchronization:** Ensure that data flows smoothly between HubSpot and the integrated platforms. This includes customer information, sales leads, marketing analytics, and any other relevant data points. A centralized data repository prevents discrepancies and improves decision-making.

4. **Automation and Workflow Optimization:** Leverage integration to automate repetitive tasks and streamline workflows. Utilize HubSpot's workflows in conjunction with other platforms to trigger actions, send notifications, and personalize interactions based on data from multiple sources.

5. **Monitoring and Analysis:** Implement monitoring tools to track the performance of integrated systems. Analyze metrics, KPIs, and user feedback to continuously optimize integration strategies for better results.

By effectively integrating HubSpot with other platforms, businesses can create a cohesive ecosystem that enhances productivity, data accuracy, and customer satisfaction.

Customizing Hubspot For Specific Business Needs

Customizing HubSpot to cater to specific business needs empowers organizations to tailor their marketing, sales, and customer service strategies for optimal outcomes. **Here are essential considerations for customizing HubSpot:**

1. **Assessing Business Requirements:** Understand the unique needs and objectives of your business. Identify pain points, specific goals, and areas that require customization within HubSpot, such as contact management, lead nurturing, or reporting functionalities.

2. **Utilizing HubSpot's Customization Features:** Take advantage of HubSpot's robust customization features, including custom properties, workflows, templates, and reports. Customize fields, create personalized templates, and design automated workflows tailored to your business processes.

3. **Personalization and Segmentation:** Leverage HubSpot's segmentation capabilities to personalize communication and marketing efforts. Use custom properties to categorize contacts based on behavior, demographics, or engagement levels, allowing for targeted and more effective campaigns.

4. **Integrating Brand Identity:** Ensure that HubSpot aligns with your brand identity by customizing email templates, landing pages, and forms. Consistent branding across all touchpoints helps in establishing a recognizable brand image.

5. **Training and Continuous Improvement:** Provide training to team members on customized features and workflows. Encourage ongoing learning and

feedback to refine and improve the customization based on evolving business needs.

Customizing HubSpot to suit specific business requirements enables a more tailored approach to marketing, sales, and customer relationship management, resulting in improved efficiency and better customer experiences.

Exploring Third-Party Integrations For Enhanced Functionality

In today's interconnected business landscape, exploring third-party integrations alongside HubSpot can unlock additional functionalities and capabilities. **Here are key aspects to consider when exploring third-party integrations:**

1. **Identifying Complementary Tools:** Research and identify third-party tools that complement HubSpot's functionalities. Look for tools that fill gaps or offer specialized features, such as social media management, analytics, customer support, or project management.

2. **Integration Compatibility:** Ensure seamless integration between HubSpot and third-party tools. Check for existing integrations or use APIs to establish connections that facilitate data flow and operational synergy.

3. **Enhancing Customer Experience:** Choose integrations that contribute to enhancing the overall customer experience. For instance, integrating live chat software or customer

support platforms can improve response times and satisfaction levels.

4. **Scalability and Flexibility:** Select integrations that are scalable and adaptable to evolving business needs. Consider tools that offer flexibility and scalability as your business grows, avoiding limitations in functionality or capacity.

5. **Cost and Return on Investment:** Evaluate the cost-effectiveness of third-party integrations. Assess the return on investment (ROI) by weighing the benefits gained from additional functionalities against the costs involved in integrating and maintaining these tools.

By exploring and implementing third-party integrations alongside HubSpot, businesses can augment their capabilities, improve operational efficiency, and deliver enhanced experiences to customers.

BEST PRACTICES FOR MAXIMIZING HUBSPOT'S POTENTIAL

Tips and Tricks for Efficiency

E fficiency is crucial in today's fast-paced world. Here are some tips and tricks to enhance productivity and streamline tasks:

1. Prioritize and Time Blocking

Prioritizing tasks is key to being efficient. Use the Eisenhower Matrix, categorizing tasks into urgent, important, non-urgent, and non-important. Time blocking involves setting specific time slots for particular tasks, reducing multitasking and increasing focus.

2. Embrace Technology

Utilize productivity tools like Trello, Asana, or Monday.com for task management and organization. Automation tools such as Zapier or IFTTT can automate repetitive tasks, saving time and effort.

3. Optimize Work Environment

A clutter-free and organized workspace boosts efficiency. Ensure ergonomic furniture, proper lighting, and minimal distractions. Consider adopting the Pomodoro Technique, working in intervals with short breaks to maintain focus.

4. Delegate and Outsource

Recognize tasks that can be delegated or outsourced to others. Delegating responsibilities not only distributes workload but also allows others to grow and learn. Outsourcing tasks like administrative work or content creation can free up time for high-priority tasks.

5. Continuous Learning and Skill Enhancement

Invest in personal development by continuously learning new skills. Attend workshops, take online courses, or read relevant literature to stay updated in your field. Acquiring new knowledge and skills can streamline processes and improve efficiency.

Avoiding Common Mistakes

Mistakes can impede progress and efficiency. Here are common errors to steer clear of in the quest for productivity:

1. Lack of Planning

Jumping into tasks without a clear plan often leads to confusion and inefficiency. Create a roadmap or outline before starting a project to ensure a smoother workflow.

2. Overcommitment

Agreeing to too many tasks or projects can spread resources thin and decrease overall efficiency. Learn to say no or negotiate deadlines to prevent burnout and maintain quality work.

3. Procrastination

Delaying tasks or waiting until the last minute increases stress and affects output quality. Combat procrastination by breaking tasks into smaller, manageable parts and setting deadlines for each.

4. Poor Communication

Miscommunication or lack of communication among team members can lead to misunderstandings, rework, and wasted time. Use clear and concise communication channels to ensure everyone is on the same page.

5. Failure to Learn from Mistakes

Repeatedly making the same mistakes without learning from them hinders progress. Reflect on past errors, analyze what went wrong, and implement strategies to avoid similar pitfalls in the future.

Leveraging Hubspot For Business Growth

HubSpot is a powerful tool for businesses aiming for growth. Here's how you can leverage HubSpot effectively:

1. Utilize CRM Features

HubSpot's Customer Relationship Management (CRM) tool

allows for centralized customer data management. Use it to track leads, manage contacts, and analyze customer interactions, enabling personalized marketing and sales efforts.

2. Marketing Automation

Take advantage of HubSpot's marketing automation features to streamline marketing campaigns. Automate email marketing, social media posting, and lead nurturing, saving time and targeting potential customers effectively.

3. Content Management and SEO

HubSpot offers content management tools and SEO guidance to improve online visibility. Create and manage content, optimize it for search engines, and analyze performance using HubSpot's analytics to refine strategies.

4. Sales Automation and Pipeline Management

Optimize sales processes by using HubSpot's sales automation features. Manage sales pipelines, automate follow-ups, and track deals to enhance sales efficiency and increase conversions.

5. Analyze and Adapt

Utilize HubSpot's analytics and reporting tools to gather insights into marketing, sales, and customer behavior. Analyze data regularly to identify trends, measure performance, and make informed decisions for continuous improvement.

Leveraging these tips and tools can significantly enhance efficiency, avoid common pitfalls, and harness the power of

HubSpot for business growth and development.

TROUBLESHOOTING AND SUPPORT

*Handling Common
Issues in HubSpot*

HubSpot, a powerful customer relationship management (CRM) platform, can encounter various common issues that users might face while navigating its features. Understanding these issues and their resolutions is crucial for seamless user experience.

1. Login and Access Problems

Users may encounter issues related to login authentication or accessing certain features within HubSpot. This could result from incorrect login credentials, browser compatibility issues, or network connectivity problems. Resolving this involves:

- **Checking Login Credentials:** Ensure the correct username and password are being used.
- **Browser Troubleshooting:** Clear cache and cookies, update the browser, or try using a

different browser to access HubSpot.

- **Network Connectivity:** Ensure a stable internet connection or switch to a different network to rule out connectivity issues.

2. Data Integration and Syncing Errors

Issues might arise when syncing data between HubSpot and other integrated platforms, causing discrepancies or missing information. To resolve these issues:

- **Check Integration Settings:** Ensure proper configuration and synchronization settings between HubSpot and other connected platforms.

- **Data Mapping Verification:** Review data mapping configurations to ensure correct fields are mapped for seamless data transfer.

- **Sync Frequency:** Adjust the sync frequency to resolve any delays or sync errors.

3. Email Deliverability and Tracking

Users may face challenges related to email deliverability or issues with tracking email opens and clicks. To troubleshoot these problems:

- **Check Email Settings:** Verify domain settings and SPF/DKIM authentication for better email deliverability.

- **Investigate Email Performance:** Analyze email engagement metrics within HubSpot to identify any tracking issues or delivery errors.

- **Review Contact Lists:** Ensure contacts have opted in to receive emails to prevent deliverability issues.

Utilizing Support Resources And

Communities

HubSpot offers extensive support resources and active communities where users can seek assistance, share insights, and troubleshoot problems collectively.

1. HubSpot Knowledge Base and Documentation

The Knowledge Base serves as a comprehensive guide containing articles, tutorials, and troubleshooting solutions. Leveraging this resource involves:

- **Search and Navigation:** Utilize the search function to find relevant articles and navigate through the documentation for step-by-step solutions.

- **Video Tutorials:** Watch video tutorials for visual guidance on using HubSpot features and resolving issues.

2. HubSpot Community Forums

Engaging with the HubSpot community forums provides access to a pool of collective knowledge and experiences. Here's how to make the most of it:

- **Ask Questions:** Post queries or issues on the forums to seek advice from experienced users and HubSpot experts.

- **Contribute and Share:** Share insights, best practices, or solutions to contribute positively to the community and help others facing similar issues.

Troubleshooting Advanced Problems

At times, users might encounter more complex issues that require in-depth troubleshooting methods beyond the basic fixes.

1. API Integration Errors

Advanced users integrating HubSpot with custom applications might encounter API-related errors. To address these issues:

- **Error Logging:** Monitor error logs and identify specific error codes to pinpoint the problem areas.
- **Check API Limits:** Ensure API usage limits are not exceeded, causing integration failures.
- **Review Code Integration:** Debug code for any syntax errors or compatibility issues affecting the API integration.

2. Workflow Automation Challenges

Users might face challenges with complex workflow automation or issues with triggers and actions not functioning as expected. Solutions involve:

- **Workflow Audit:** Review and analyze the workflow setup to identify any misconfigured actions or triggers.
- **Testing and Debugging:** Test workflows with sample data to identify and resolve automation bottlenecks or errors.
- **Consult HubSpot Support:** Reach out to HubSpot support for guidance on intricate workflow automation issues.

CONCLUSION

*Encouragement for Ongoing
Learning and Improvement
with HubSpot*

HubSpot, renowned for its versatile marketing, sales, and customer service tools, offers an extensive array of resources to foster continuous learning and improvement. Here, we delve into the strategies and incentives that can inspire individuals and businesses to embrace ongoing learning within the HubSpot ecosystem.

1. Diverse Learning Channels

HubSpot's commitment to ongoing learning manifests through diverse learning channels. From comprehensive documentation and detailed video tutorials to live webinars and interactive workshops, **these various avenues** ensure that users can engage with content in ways that suit their learning preferences.

Exploration:

- **Documentation:** Detailed guides and articles catering to different skill levels facilitate self-paced learning.
- **Video Tutorials:** Engaging and visually appealing tutorials offer step-by-step guidance on using HubSpot tools effectively.
- **Live Webinars:** Interactive sessions led by experts offer real-time insights and Q&A opportunities.
- **Workshops:** Hands-on workshops empower users to apply their knowledge in practical scenarios.

2. Gamification and Challenges

Incorporating gamification elements and challenges into the learning process can significantly enhance motivation and engagement. HubSpot can leverage this strategy by introducing **gamified learning modules** and **skill-based challenges**.

Exploration:

- **Badges and Rewards:** Offering badges or certificates upon completion of modules can acknowledge progress and incentivize continuous learning.
- **Leaderboards:** Introducing leaderboards showcasing top performers can create healthy competition and motivate users.
- **Challenges and Quizzes:** Periodic challenges or quizzes can reinforce learning and encourage active participation.

3. Personalized Learning Paths

Tailoring learning paths based on individual preferences and goals can amplify the learning experience. HubSpot's platform could offer **personalized recommendations** and **customized learning tracks** to address specific skill gaps.

Exploration:

- **Assessment Tools:** Evaluating user proficiency can help in suggesting relevant learning materials.

- **Customizable Modules:** Allowing users to create their own learning paths based on their interests and objectives.

- **Progress Tracking:** Providing insights into progress made and suggesting next steps can keep users motivated.

4. Community Engagement and Collaboration

Creating a vibrant community where users can share insights, collaborate, and seek guidance fosters an environment conducive to ongoing learning. HubSpot can facilitate this through **online forums**, **dedicated groups**, and **mentorship programs**.

Exploration:

- **Forums and Discussion Boards:** Platforms for users to ask questions, share experiences, and seek advice from peers and experts.

- **User Groups:** Building communities centered around specific industries or interests to encourage networking and knowledge exchange.

- **Mentorship Initiatives:** Pairing experienced users with newcomers can accelerate learning and skill development.

5. Continuous Updates and Learning Material Expansion

HubSpot's commitment to ongoing improvement should reflect in regular updates to its platform and learning materials. Keeping content **fresh, relevant**, and **up-to-date** ensures users are equipped with the latest knowledge and tools.

Exploration:

- **Platform Updates:** Regularly introducing new features and improvements that align with industry trends.

- **Content Refresh:** Revising existing content and adding new resources to cater to evolving user needs.

- **Feedback Loop:** Encouraging user feedback to understand learning gaps and adapting content accordingly.

6. Recognition and Success Stories

Highlighting success stories and recognizing users who have excelled through their continuous learning journey can serve as powerful motivators. HubSpot can feature **case studies, success stories**, and **spotlight interviews** to inspire others.

Exploration:

- **Customer Spotlights:** Showcasing how businesses have leveraged HubSpot to achieve their goals.

- **Success Metrics:** Sharing measurable outcomes and achievements resulting from learning and utilizing HubSpot.

- **User Testimonials:** Amplifying positive user experiences to encourage others to follow suit.